INDIVIDUAL DEVELOPMENT PLAN 2.0

INDIVIDUAL DEVELOPMENT PLAN 2.0

Master Your Professional Development
in 4 Practical Steps

GONZALO CORDOVA

LEADERSHIP HOLDINGS LLC

Copyright © 2020 Gonzalo Cordova

All rights reserved.

No part of this work may be reproduced or transmitted in any form or by any means, electronic or mechanical, including photocopying and recording, or by any information storage or retrieval system, except as may be expressly permitted by the 1976 Copyright Act or in writing from the publisher. Requests for permission can be addressed to permissions@LeadershipHoldingsLLC.com.

ISBN 978-1-7349088-0-0 (Hardcover)
ISBN 978-1-7349088-1-7 (Paperback)
ISBN 978-1-7349088-2-4 (eBook)

Library of Congress Control Number: 2020906716

The author and publisher of this handbook disclaim any liability or responsibility for loss or damage, personal or otherwise, resulting from the direct or indirect use and application of this handbook or the information, ideas, or opinions contained within.

Editing by Ami McConnell and Lori Jones

Cover and interior designs by Kristen Ingebretson

20 21 22 23 24 25 26 27 28 29 — 10 9 8 7 6 5 4 3 2 1

MANUFACTURED IN THE UNITED STATES OF AMERICA

Published by Leadership Holdings LLC
www.LeadershipHoldingsLLC.com

For my Support Crew.

I could not go the distance without you!

CONTENTS

Introduction	11
Fundamentals	15
A Customized Approach	19
Step 1. Assessing Your Capabilities	23
Step 2. Setting Your Long-Term Professional Goals	29
Step 3. Identifying Meaningful Capabilities	35
Step 4. Committing to Tangible Actions and Metrics	41
Final Notes	47
Appendix: Individual Development Plan 2.0 Quick Guide	51
Acknowledgments	53
About the Author	55

INTRODUCTION

As an engineer who puts a high value on processes and systems, I am a highly organized person, and it's no secret I keep a tight calendar. But over the years I've developed a real passion and joy for helping young professionals navigate the tricky road we call a career path. So even when my schedule is full, I often agree spontaneously to meet with those who seek some advice.

Just today a young man stopped by to see me, seeking help with his professional development. I invited him right in. He'd brought a copy of a beautifully typed-up plan for professional development and asked me to review it. He even offered to email me a digital copy. Right away I could tell that this guy was organized and driven. He was also respectful, assuring me he appreciated the value of my time. I respected that. But when I asked him how he came up with his plan, he started to fidget a little. His response was vague, in line with what I typically hear from young professionals. It's often something like:

- "My manager recommended it."
- "People above me in my organization have these skills, so I guess I need them too."
- "A friend I admire is working on these areas."
- "I read that these skills are crucial for leaders."

What was missing from his plan was passion and initiative. The goals he was setting weren't based on his own interests and strengths—they were all based on external sources. It was clear to me that he had work yet to do.

PROFESSIONAL GROWTH

We all know that professional development is valuable. We acknowledge that it's something we "should" do, like eat our vegetables and exercise. Most of us make some attempt at it, however, very few do it effectively and therefore the "development" isn't fruitful or productive. I know this from personal experience. When I started out in my career, I had big dreams. I was highly motivated and had the best intentions to develop professionally toward my long-term goals, but despite my efforts, I made very slow progress. I read extensively, hoping to find a way forward, but the books I read assumed—incorrectly—that I already knew what I needed to work on.

Fast forward almost a decade later. After lots of trial and error, I was fortunate to be mentored by some experienced leaders. Learning from them, I developed an efficient way to manage my professional development and achieved many of my long-term goals. I've refined the framework I developed over the years into what I now call the Individual Development Plan 2.0. As I've mentored and coached others through this plan, it's proven to be a powerful and effective tool for both personal and professional development. What's more, it's customizable, so users can create their own unique path toward their own vision of success. It has been tremendously gratifying for me to see young professionals use the *Individual Development Plan 2.0* to move from confusion to clarity and from frustration to satisfaction, and I'm excited to share this plan with you.

FUNDAMENTALS

While the *Individual Development Plan 2.0* is quite simple, the four steps of the *Individual Development Plan 2.0* build directly upon four fundamental truths.

1. YOU ARE THE CEO OF YOUR OWN CAREER

You are the boss of your own professional development. Many people I've mentored and coached over the years erroneously expected their managers, mentors, or coaches to assume this responsibility, but the truth is you are the driver of your career. No one in the world is more invested in your success than you are. Ultimately, you alone are the boss of your career development. So instead of thinking of your boss, your coach, or your manager as responsible for you, consider them as consultants who can offer input along the way.

2. SELF-REFLECTION IS KEY

Growing and developing professionally is time-consuming work, both intellectually and emotionally strenuous. But perhaps the most important aspect of this journey is that it requires you take the time for genuine self-reflection. There is no shortcut for this. Tough questions must be asked and honest answers given to maximize one's professional potential and reach long-term goals.

3. COMPETENCE ISN'T ENOUGH

I've seen many young professionals get discouraged because they believed someone in upper management would tap them for a promotion simply for doing a "good job." But doing your job well is not enough to accelerate your career journey. Growth doesn't happen when we sit still. Professional development takes effort. Every successful person can look back and say they began their career with zero experience, and they progressed only through a series of successes and mistakes. A savvy professional learns to make the most of this process and keep pushing forward.

4. YOU NEED MEASURABLE OUTCOMES

Regardless of the method you choose to approach your career development, you need to be able to measure your progress in a tangible way. I have found that vague metrics regarding career development allow people to feel good about their progress, even though no gains are noticeable. The good news is that establishing tangible metrics to track career development progress is not complicated and allows you to have meaningful career progression conversations with your managers, mentors, and coaches. Candid career conversations are possible when your goals and motives are clear and you can objectively measure progress.

A CUSTOMIZED APPROACH

In the *Individual Development Plan 2.0*, I share with you a process that will help you identify your areas of opportunity based on who you are today relative to who you want to be professionally in the long term. With the output from the *Individual Development Plan 2.0*, you'll have a roadmap to success with tangible and measurable milestones (Figure 1).

Figure 1: Individual Development Plan 2.0 Overview

INDIVIDUAL DEVELOPMENT PLAN 2.0

No assumptions are made. You're the boss. You will establish your baseline, your long-term goals, and your customized path to success through four simple steps:

1. ASSESSING YOUR CAPABILITIES
2. SETTING YOUR LONG-TERM PROFESSIONAL GOALS
3. IDENTIFYING MEANINGFUL CAPABILITIES
4. COMMITTING TO TANGIBLE ACTIONS AND METRICS

In the following chapters of this handbook, you will find a comprehensive description of the four steps of the *Individual Development Plan 2.0*, including an example of the expected output for each step and a template to apply what you've learned.

STEP 1

ASSESSING YOUR CAPABILITIES

The first step involves the most self-reflection and asks you to assess the professional and the person you are today. In this step, you will rank your capabilities and expertise using two metrics: your level of mastery and how much you enjoy using those capabilities. The key tool for this step is the Capability Assessment Matrix depicted in Figure 2.

Figure 2: Capability Assessment Matrix

GET REAL

Completing the Capability Assessment Matrix requires full honesty and a lot of self-reflection. Remember, you are the boss. There's no need to try to impress or fool anyone. The goal is to get a realistic assessment of where you stand today.

EXTRACURRICULAR ACTIVITIES

When I use this tool in my coaching and mentoring, I recommend expanding the scope of capabilities in this matrix beyond the professional realm. Consider other abilities you have that you enjoy outside of the workplace. If you are fortunate enough to have a manager, mentor, or coach supporting your career development, sharing these extra-work capabilities will help them better understand you as a whole person. For example, knowing that you like and are good at painting landscapes would help your coach or mentor to understand that you have a creative edge that could support the development of other capabilities. Share as much as you feel comfortable given the level of trust you have developed with your mentor.

ROOM TO GROW

In initial drafts of the Capability Assessment Matrix, people often populate the quadrants on the top tier quickly because it's often easier to think of things we like and are good at. Can you guess what happens with the quadrant showing the capabilities we both dislike and/or have not mastered yet? Yep, this is the least populated area, but one that is crucial for seeing where you have the most opportunity for growth. If you get stuck in this section, I recommend asking someone you trust who knows you well to help identify the areas where you need to improve. I have found this very helpful personally. You will be surprised on how quickly the list grows when you ask those close to you for feedback.

SEEING IS BELIEVING

To get your thoughts flowing, here are a few examples of capabilities you may consider for your own matrix:

ASSESSING YOUR CAPABILITIES

- Analytical skills
- Public speaking
- Leading high-performing teams
- Concise communication
- Professional savvy
- Strategic thinking
- Networking
- Project management
- Developing others
- Work-life balance

If you are looking for other capabilities that resonate with you, books I like to recommend are *FYI: For Your Improvement—Competencies Development Guide* by Heather Barnfield and Michael Lombardo and *Compass: Your Guide for Leadership Development and Coaching* by Peter Scisco, Elaine Biech, and George Hallenbeck. Consulting your managers and prior performance reviews or 360 degree evaluations can also help you identify a list of capabilities you can use to populate the Capability Assessment Matrix. Just keep in mind that other people's assessments are not the final word. Again, you are the CEO of your career.

Figure 3 gives you a hypothetical example of a completed Capability Assessment Matrix. This example is not intended to prescribe the content for you. The right content for your Capability Assessment Matrix is unique to you—only you will know how best to populate it. This is simply a hypothetical example to give you a tangible representation of the ideas discussed above.

INDIVIDUAL DEVELOPMENT PLAN 2.0

Figure 3: Hypothetical Capability Assessment Matrix

TIME TO DIVE IN

I invite you to apply what you learned in this chapter by populating your own Capability Assessment Matrix (Figure 4). Remember that quality trumps speed in this exercise.

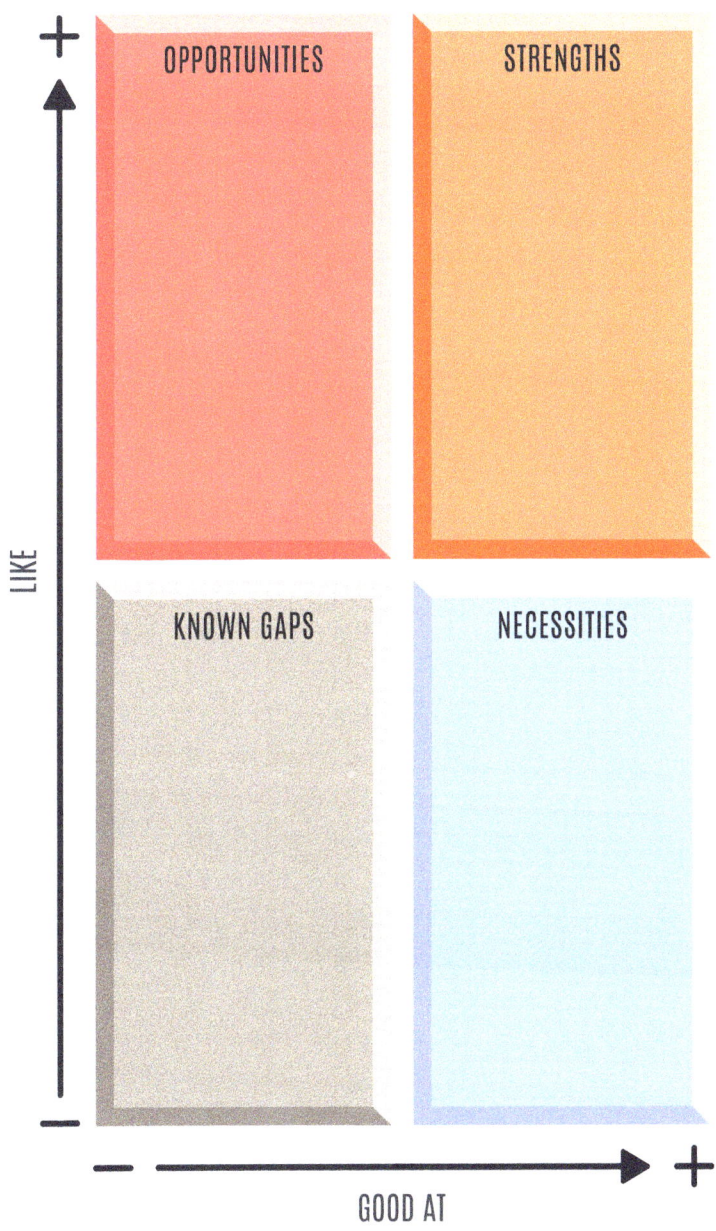

Figure 4: Your Capability Assessment Matrix

STEP 2

SETTING YOUR LONG-TERM PROFESSIONAL GOALS

In order to safely arrive at a desired destination, you have to first know where you're going. That's what we're doing when we set goals—we're determining our destination. As the boss of your own career development, you get to define specific long-term professional goals that will fulfill your personal career aspirations. No one can answer this for you—and that's the beauty of it! It is exhilarating to ask yourself who you want to be.

CLOSE YOUR EYES

Picture yourself at your retirement party. Imagine that someone you respect introduces you to the crowd and acknowledges your reputation and professional accomplishments. You feel proud of what you hear. You smile and acknowledge that, in fact, you are the person being described. It feels good. What is he or she saying about you? The accolades this imaginary speaker gives you in this "dream" are your long-term goals.

HOLD YOUR GOALS WITH OPEN HANDS

This step is probably the most challenging one. After all, it requires you to answer the question of who you want to be when you grow up—at least professionally speaking. It can be hard to face that you are in charge of your own destiny. Since this task can become overwhelming, I would encourage you to first focus on what you know today and get started. These are your long-term goals, and since there is no immediate hurry to meet them, you can change them later as needed.

Additionally, even with a crystal-clear picture of your long-term goals, it's important to remember that your goals will change as you experience life. I will give you a personal example. Initially one of my long-term goals was that I'd work in private equity. However, after working in a world related to private equity, I realized that this goal was not aligned with my personal preferences. I found the working hours long and unpredictable and the culture wasn't a good fit for me. Thus, that initial long-term goal was no longer relevant for me and I took it off my list.

REALITY CHECK

You need to believe you can achieve your long-term professional goals, so they need to be realistic and attainable. Don't sell yourself short or set the bar too low. Think big! But, as the boss of your own career, you should be setting yourself up for success, not frustration. For example, if you landed your first job out of school in a Fortune 500 company, it is okay to set your long-term goal to be the CEO of that company within the next thirty years. However, if you state the same goal with a five-year timeframe in mind, your likelihood of achieving your goal is very low.

Also, don't be afraid to think outside of the box as you develop your long-term professional goals. Invest quality time in creating a comprehensive inventory of your professional aspirations. Asking help from people who know you well can be helpful in this step. I once coached a bright professional in a financial role who, after thinking a lot about his long-term goals, realized that his passions aligned more with music and creativity and less with the financial world. He now works for a record label, has nothing to do with financials, and truly enjoys his newfound career.

THE RULE OF THREE

Once you've created a comprehensive list of aspirations, it's time to cull the list. I recommend you limit your long-term professional goals to a maximum of three options. I offer you three reasons for this limit. First, it forces you to prioritize what is really important to you. Second, it allows you to focus your limited resources into fewer options in order to maximize your chances of achieving them. Third, you will face less complexity in the next step of the framework.

SEEING IS BELIEVING

Here are some examples of long-term professional goals I see often (in no particular order):

- Professor
- Government leader
- Business executive
- Business owner
- Independent consultant
- Subject matter expert

Figure 5 aims to give you a tangible idea of the output from step two of the framework.

Figure 5: Hypothetical Long-Term Professional Goals

TIME TO DIVE IN

Take the time to search deep within yourself to identify those long-term professional goals that most appeal to you. Write your long-term professional goals in Figure 6 below.

Figure 6: Your Long-Term Professional Goals

STEP 3
IDENTIFY MEANINGFUL CAPABILITIES

In the last step you envisioned realizing your professional aspirations at your retirement party. You engaged your imagination to discover your destination. Knowing your destination is critical because, without a destination, we tend to wander. And it's nearly impossible to arrive at a desirable destination without purposefully trying to get there, so you have to plan ahead.

In this step, you will use the outputs from the previous two steps to identify what I call **Meaningful Capabilities**. Each of us has numerous capabilities that need to be developed, but in this case we're speaking specifically of those that can move you toward your long-term goal destination.

ROCKS IN THE STREAM

Imagine you are walking a path. The path ends at the edge of a swiftly moving stream. A friend calls out to you from the other side, and you decide to cross so you can visit with your friend. The stream isn't deep, and there are a number of flat-topped rocks on which you can step. As you begin to make your way across, the question soon arises: Which stones should you choose to step on to make your way? Likely you will choose the ones that offer the strongest, most sure footing. Consider these stones your Meaningful Capabilities. They will offer you sure footing as you make your way toward your desired destination.

As you consider your career stepping stones, focus on those that can enable you to achieve your long-term professional goals identified in Step Two. Your career stepping stones are a subset of the capabilities that you identified in your Capability Assessment Matrix as Opportunities. These are capabilities that fall into the upper left quadrant—those you like but are not yet good at—in the Capability Assessment Matrix. This is where I recommend you start. Developing any new capability presents unique challenges, so I believe you might as well like the topic you are working on!

If possible, pick capabilities that will move you closer to all three of your long-term professional goals. Such multi-purpose capabilities can reasonably be called "no regret" capabilities because regardless of how your career progresses, the development of these capabilities will not be wasted.

RULE OF THREE

Again, limit the number of meaningful capabilities you will develop to a maximum of three. This limit will help you focus your efforts on developing those capabilities you are most interested in. Additionally, limiting the number of capabilities you are developing will increase your chances of making an impact on your professional development with limited resources.

PROGRESS BUILDS MUSCLE

If you're very goal-driven, choosing three capabilities to develop may feel daunting, like you have to choose the right answer. But rest assured, there is no wrong answer. Even if you ultimately don't use a particular capability to thrive in your dream position, you won't regret the effort. As with cross-training for the body, learning and growing is never wasted!

BUY-IN FROM TRUSTED ADVISORS

If you are fortunate enough to have a manager, coach, or mentor involved in your professional development, it's wise to check in with them about these capabilities you plan to cultivate. They have the advantage of seeing your professional development needs from a different perspective, and this can be very valuable to the process. However, remember that you are the driver of your career. You should take their recommendations seriously, but they do not have the final word. You do. When you take responsibility for your decisions about what capabilities you want to grow, you'll be more motivated to follow through.

SEEING IS BELIEVING

The following is a hypothetical example of Identifying Meaningful Capabilities (Figure 7). I have chosen three meaningful capabilities from the "like" and "not-good-at" quadrant in the Capability Assessment Matrix example presented earlier. Notice these capabilities are "meaningful" because they align with the long-term professional goals from Step Two (i.e., they mean something to this hypothetical profession). All could clearly facilitate the three long-term professional goals, thus, these are also "no-regret" capabilities.

Figure 7: Hypothetical Example of Meaningful Capabilities

TIME TO DIVE IN

Using your Capability Assessment Matrix from Step One and your Long-Term Professional Goals from Step Two, identify your top three Meaningful Capabilities. Document your meaningful capabilities in Figure 8 below.

Figure 8: Your Meaningful Capabilities

STEP 4

COMMITTING TO TANGIBLE ACTIONS AND METRICS

Now that you've invested the time in self-reflection and taken an inventory of the capabilities in need of development that can move you toward your professional goals, it's time to act. The fourth step is designed to transform your Meaningful Capabilities into Outstanding Features, such as those attributes that would be applauded in your ideal retirement party. The way you increase these capabilities is by taking tangible actions.

LOOK FOR TANGIBLE IMPACT

In your professional development, others will look for quantifiable proof that you are more than qualified. That's why it's important that each of your professional development steps are tangible. You and others will be able to point to them as substantial and real.

For example, a young professional I coached was extremely competent at her job, but she needed to overcome her fear of public speaking in order to progress in her career. She joined an organization that helped her hone her public speaking skills, gained confidence, and was soon noticed by upper management. These were tangible, noticeable improvements.

DO YOUR RESEARCH

Invest some time in researching ideas about how to improve a certain capability. Managers, coaches, and mentors can be helpful with this step as well. As with of Step One, you may also consider using the books *FYI: For Your Improvement—Competencies Development Guide* by Heather Barnfield and Michael Lombardo and *Compass: Your Guide for Leadership Development and Coaching* by Peter Scisco, Elaine Biech, and George Hallenbeck as guides.

THE RULE OF THREE

Limit yourself to no more than three actions at one time to improve each selected Meaningful Capability. Limiting the scope will help you move the needle more quickly, keep you motivated, and help you see progress.

METRICS

Actions with measurable outcomes are more likely to yield results, so assign metrics to track your progress. Such metrics should be simple. For example, if you've decided to read strategy articles to improve your strategic thinking, the metric to be used could be quantity of articles (or the amount of time spent reading articles) per week. Set these goals for yourself and then track them. Periodic tracking of the metrics is a way to hold yourself accountable, so make checking in on those part of your weekly or monthly routines.

SEEING IS BELIEVING

To conclude the description of this step, see Figure 9 below, which expands the hypothetical example of Meaningful Capabilities from Step Three. Note that the developmental actions are tangible and the metrics allow the tracking of the outputs in a simple way. Remember that these developmental actions and metrics are generic and serve only to illustrate the final output of the framework.

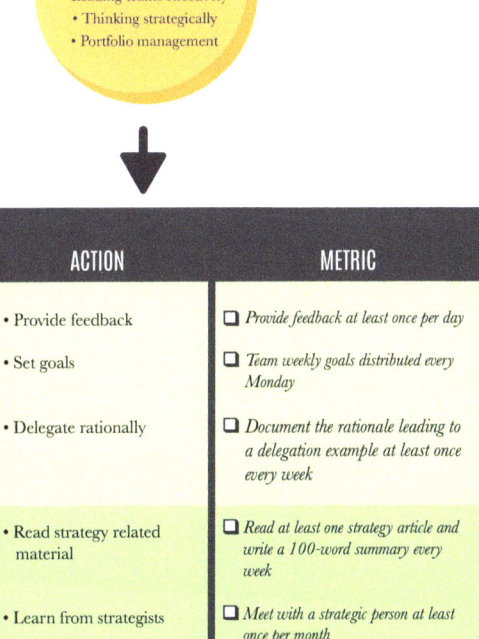

Figure 9: Example of Tangible Developmental Actions and Metrics

TIME TO DIVE IN

For your three Meaningful Capabilities identified in Step Three, select the actions that you will take to in order to develop them and the metrics you will use to track progress. Use Figure 10 below to document your tangible actions and metrics.

Figure 10: Your Tangible Developmental Actions and Metrics

FINAL THOUGHTS

When the young professionals I coach complete their individual development plan using the *Individual Development Plan 2.0* framework, they take one of two paths:

- They act on what they've learned immediately, or
- They postpone taking action to a future time for multiple reasons.

Sadly, the ones in the latter group very rarely start the execution of the individual development plan. As a result, they are unlikely to make the progress they desire. To arrive at a destination, you have to start the journey!

PRIORITIZE TO SUCCEED

I would encourage you to maximize the value of your strategic individual development plan by making its execution part of your weekly routine. One of the best practices I have found is to block time on my calendar for this purpose. Treat this time as any other mandatory appointment that must get done. When schedule conflicts occur, reschedule your professional development time instead of simply cancelling the appointment.

START WHERE YOU ARE

Even if you hope to make a professional or career change soon, first look for opportunities to develop professionally in your current job. It is hard to find jobs that perfectly match the development of your meaningful capabilities, but you will be surprised by how much professional development you can extract from your current job and its responsibilities if you are creative and purposeful. When you are given the opportunity for a new position or role, consider those roles carefully based on their alignment with the meaningful capabilities you are trying to develop.

TRACK PROGRESS

In terms of maintenance of your individual development plan, I recommend updating it once per year. As you evolve as a person and as a professional, your preferences and long-term professional goals will evolve as well. Also, in most companies, there is an annual performance review cycle, which is a great opportunity to receive feedback about the capabilities you should work on. In between annual updates, I recommend updating your individual development plan only when you master a Meaningful Capability and are ready to take upon the next one on the list. Before defining a new Meaningful Capability to work on in Step Three, do a self-check regarding your long-term goals. Only you can judge if these goals are still relevant. Update them as needed. Keeping these long-term goals fresh ensures you're on the right path. This self-check is bound to invigorate your appetite to work on your next Meaningful Capability.

HERE'S TO YOU!

I invite you to take a few moments to internalize what you have accomplished by reading through how to implement this *Individual Development Plan 2.0*. Your time is precious, and in

FINAL THOUGHTS

reading and internalizing this information, you've invested wisely and well. Just imagine: you are now armed with a tool to identify key areas of opportunity, specifically tailored to who you are and where you are today. You can now develop those capabilities efficiently, in a tangible way, based on your long-term professional aspirations.

It is my sincere hope that the application of this knowledge helps you enjoy a very successful career, culminating in the achievement of your hard-won, long-term goal(s).

APPENDIX: INDIVIDUAL DEVELOPMENT PLAN 2.0 QUICK GUIDE

1. ASSESS YOUR CAPABILITIES

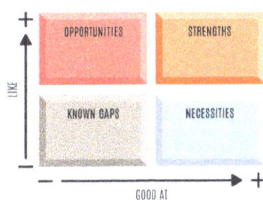

KEY CONCEPTS
- Be honest
- Allow enough time for self-reflection
- Include extracurricular activities
- Validate with someone who knows you well

2. SET LONG-TERM PROFESSIONAL GOALS

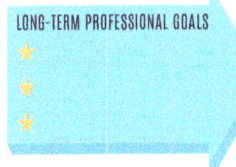

KEY CONCEPTS
- Imagine your retirement party
- Focus on what you know today
- Think big, but keep your long-term goals realistic
- Rule of three

3. IDENTIFY MEANINGFUL CAPABILITIES

KEY CONCEPTS
- Start with the like/not-good quadrant
- Rule of three
- Aim for no-regret capabilities
- Align with manager/mentor/coach

4. COMMIT TO TANGIBLE ACTIONS AND METRICS

KEY CONCEPTS
- Results must be tangible
- Do proper research to define actions and metrics
- Rule of three
- Practice and measure progress constantly

ACKNOWLEDGMENTS

It definitely takes a village! I could not have completed this handbook without the help and encouragement of a lot of people who generously shared their time, patience, and professional advice with me.

First of all, thanks to my family. I am humbled to experience life with such a loving and understanding wife and beautiful children. You challenge me to be my best version of myself every day. Thank you for believing in me and supporting every one of my multiple projects, regardless of how crazy they sound.

Mom and Rosita, sister by choice, thanks for lending a listening ear whenever I need one. I cherish your love, patience, and wisdom.

Dad, you never left. Thanks for teaching me to serve others unconditionally.

Also, thanks from the bottom of my heart to the managers, coaches, and mentors who took interest in my professional development. You helped me understand the value of improving upon my opportunities and your great ideas helped me become a better professional. Your time is valuable, so please know you made a difference in my career and life by sharing it with me.

Finally, thanks to the fantastic group of professionals who shared their time and unique talents to make this handbook a reality. Ami McConnell, Lori Jones, Kristen Ingebretson, and

Penny Sansevieri, I am in awe of how much you know about writing, designing, and publishing books. However, what I admire the most is your willingness to help others using your special gifts. It was a real pleasure working with every one of you. Rodrigo Silva, my good friend and trustworthy attorney at the service of our community. Your legal advice was instrumental to publish this handbook. I treasure our friendship.

ABOUT THE AUTHOR

Gonzalo Cordova discovered early in life a passion for continuous improvement, which led him to become an engineer with focus on optimization of processes and systems. As his career evolved, his passion for continuous improvement intersected with his desire to serve people. Hence, he now devotes a meaningful amount of his time to mentoring other professionals who desire to advance their careers. Additionally, Gonzalo is a long-distance triathlete and an avid reader. He enjoys spending quality time with his wife and two children in the northern suburbs of Atlanta, Georgia.

www.ingramcontent.com/pod-product-compliance
Lightning Source LLC
Chambersburg PA
CBHW042130100526
44587CB00026B/4246